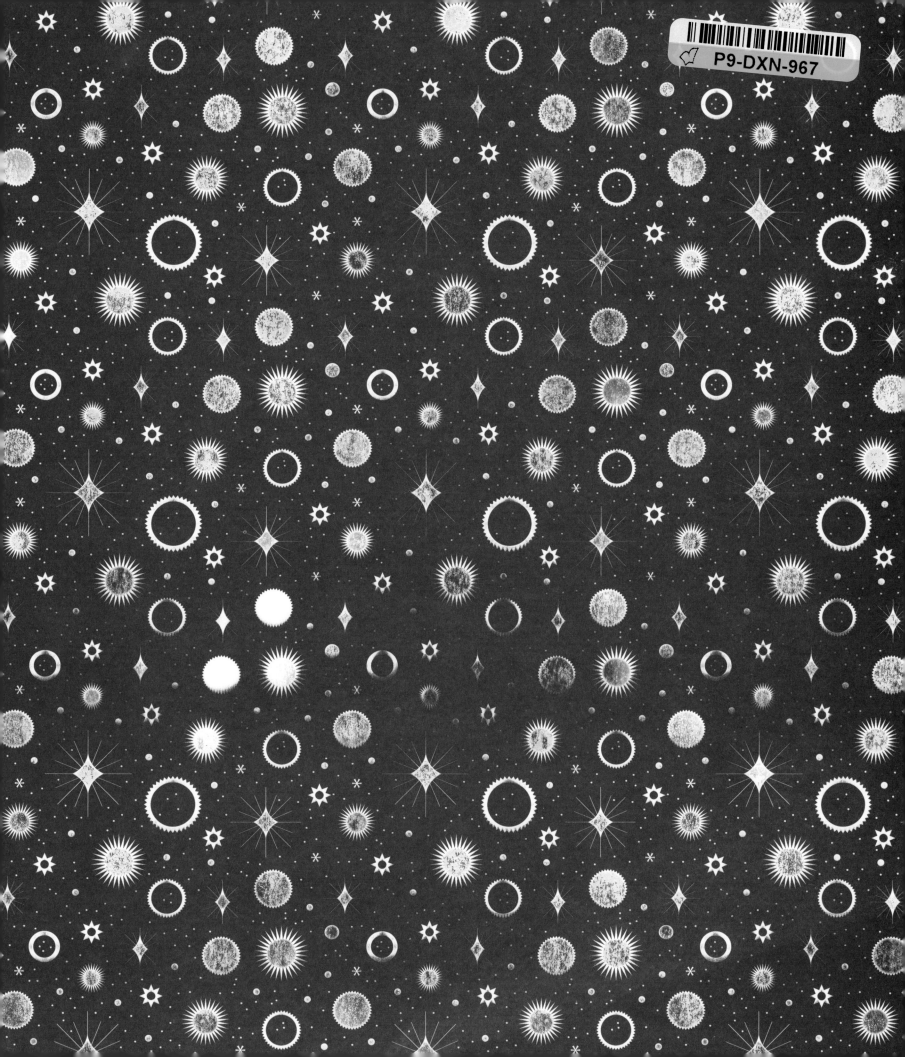

With love, for La, a true star.
With thanks again to Paul for showing me how a star is born. —J.C.

To the light of the stars that allows all magic to happen.
To Jordi, my parents, and friends, because they are a
part of this magic. —M.H.

Text copyright © 2018 by James Carter

Cover art and interior illustrations copyright © 2018 by Mar Hernández

All rights reserved. Published in the United States by Doubleday, an imprint of Random
House Children's Books, a division of Penguin Random House LLC, New York.

Originally published in the United Kingdom by Little Tiger Press, London, in 2018.

Doubleday and the colophon are registered trademarks of Penguin Random House LLC.

Visit us on the Web! rhcbooks.com

Educators and librarians, for a variety of teaching tools, visit us at
RHTeachersLibrarians.com

Library of Congress Cataloging-in-Publication Data is available upon request.

ISBN 978-0-525-57933-5

MANUFACTURED IN CHINA

10 9 8 7 6 5 4 3 2 1

First American Edition

Random House Children's Books supports the First Amendment and
celebrates the right to read.

CPB/1400/0752/1117

Once Upon a Star

A poetic journey through space

James Carter

Illustrated by

Mar Hernández

Doubleday Books for Young Readers

As the lid is lifted off the **world**,
the day goes quiet, **dark**, and **cold**.

Then
down
comes
night
and
if
cloud-
free,
look
up,
you'll
find
the galaxy.

One hundred billion, maybe more,
lights like lanterns on a shore.
GIANTS
they are
and from so far

they just seem small.
We call them

STARS.

And we have one—

it's called **THE SUN.**

But did you know it's where we're from?

There's more of that, as you'll soon see.

Now let's head back through history. . . .

Once upon a star,

there were no stars to shine—

no sun to rise,

no sun to set,

no day, no night,

nor any time.

There was no Earth

(nor universe)

until a great explosion burst!

A mighty **BOOM**

a huge **KERRANG**

that scientists call

THE
BIG
BANG!

So, then what?

EVERYTHING!

As

all of

space and

time began,

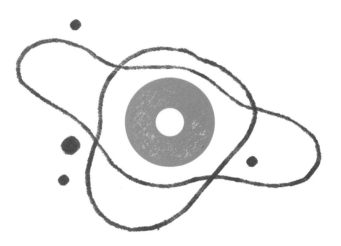

very

s l o w l y,

first of all,

the **universe**

had to cool.

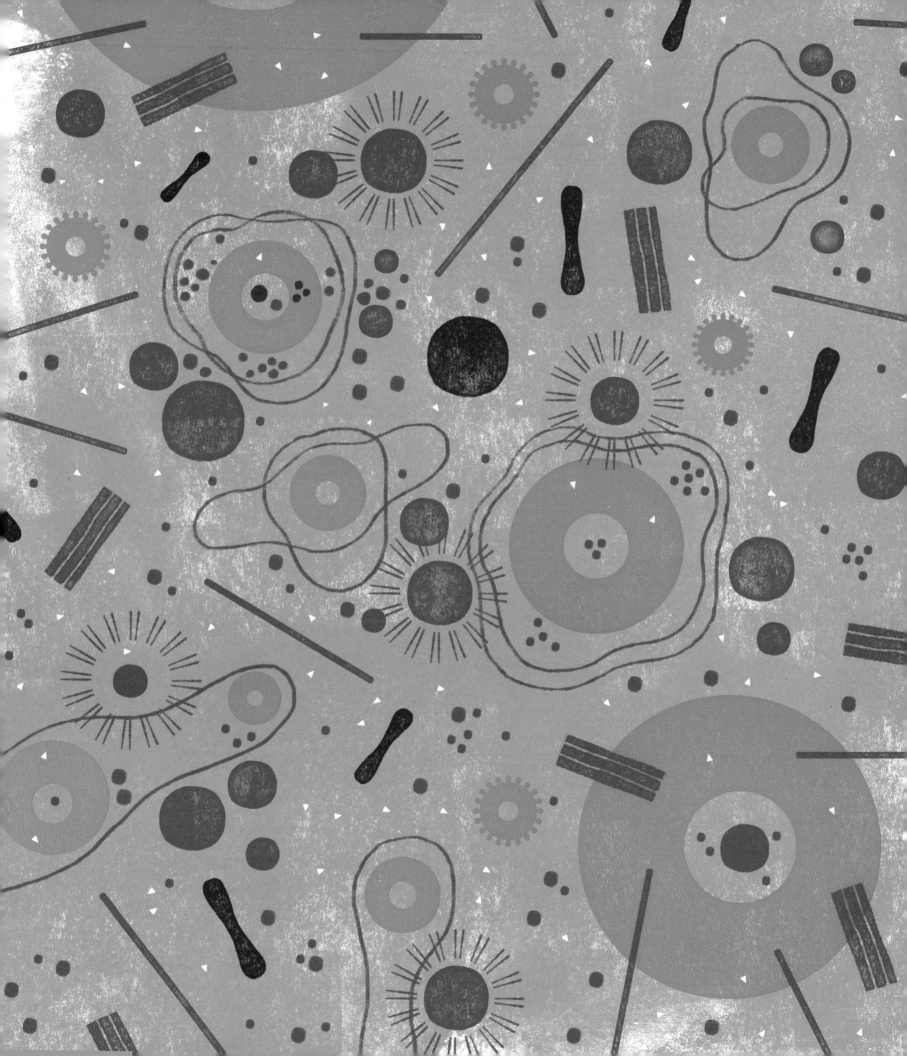

A sea of stars at last were born.

Gradually, they **fired and formed**

out of **clouds** of dust and **gas,**

each a **mighty,** sparky **mass.**

And one of these became our sun.

Our solar system had begun!

Giant rocks

and **fire blew,**

and so in time

our planets grew.

And right down here
our Earth did too!

With skies so wide

and oceans blue.

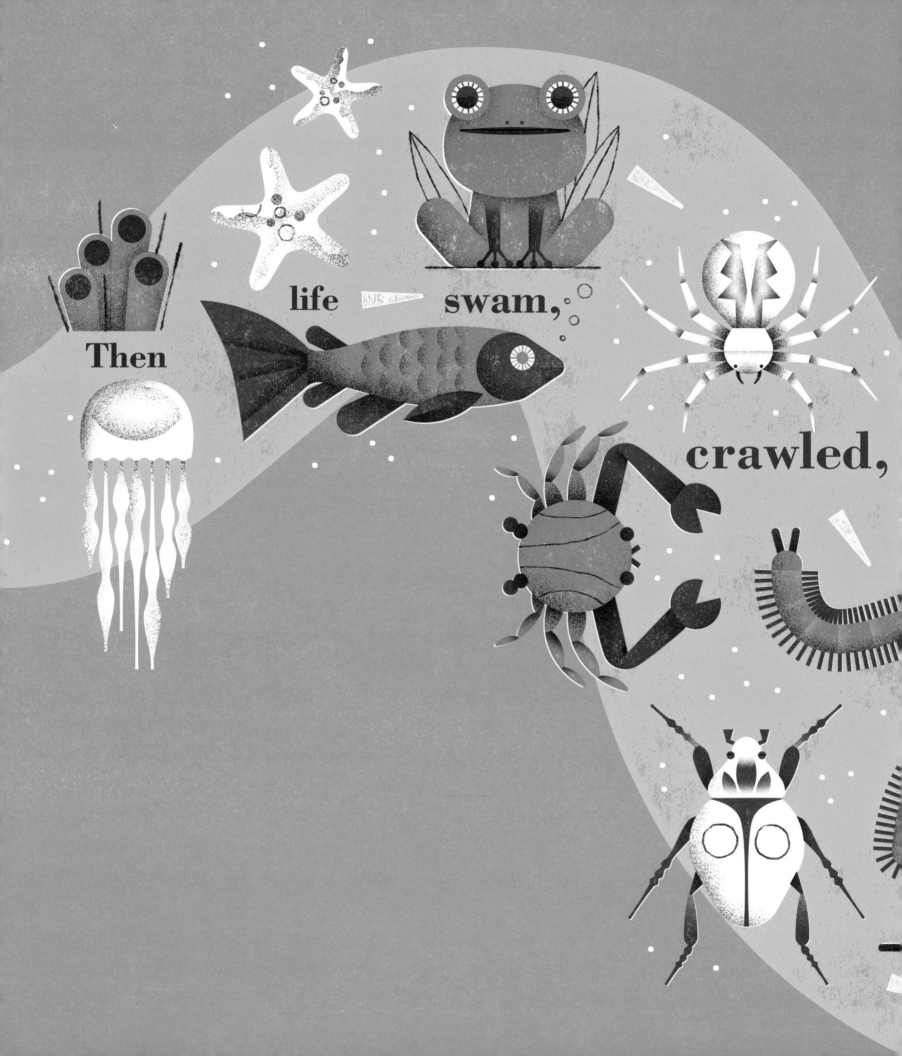

Then life swam, crawled,

flew.

And still our sun
gives us delight:
our warmth,
our food,
our daily light.

It's at the heart of everything. Around the sun the planets spin.

We're from that star
that seems so far.
We're made of stardust,
yes, we are.

So, what are you?

YOU'RE A STAR!

Sciencey Stuff

The sun, our star, was born in a nebula almost five billion years ago.

Huge amounts of gas and dust began to form a cloud.

Eventually, as the cloud grew bigger, gravity caused it to whirl and flatten.

Spinning around, it formed a clump in the center—a protostar—which would become our sun.

Ultimately, five billion years into the future, our sun will finally collapse.

Near the end of its life, the sun will eat up Mercury, Venus, and even Earth—as it becomes a massive superstar known as a RED GIANT!

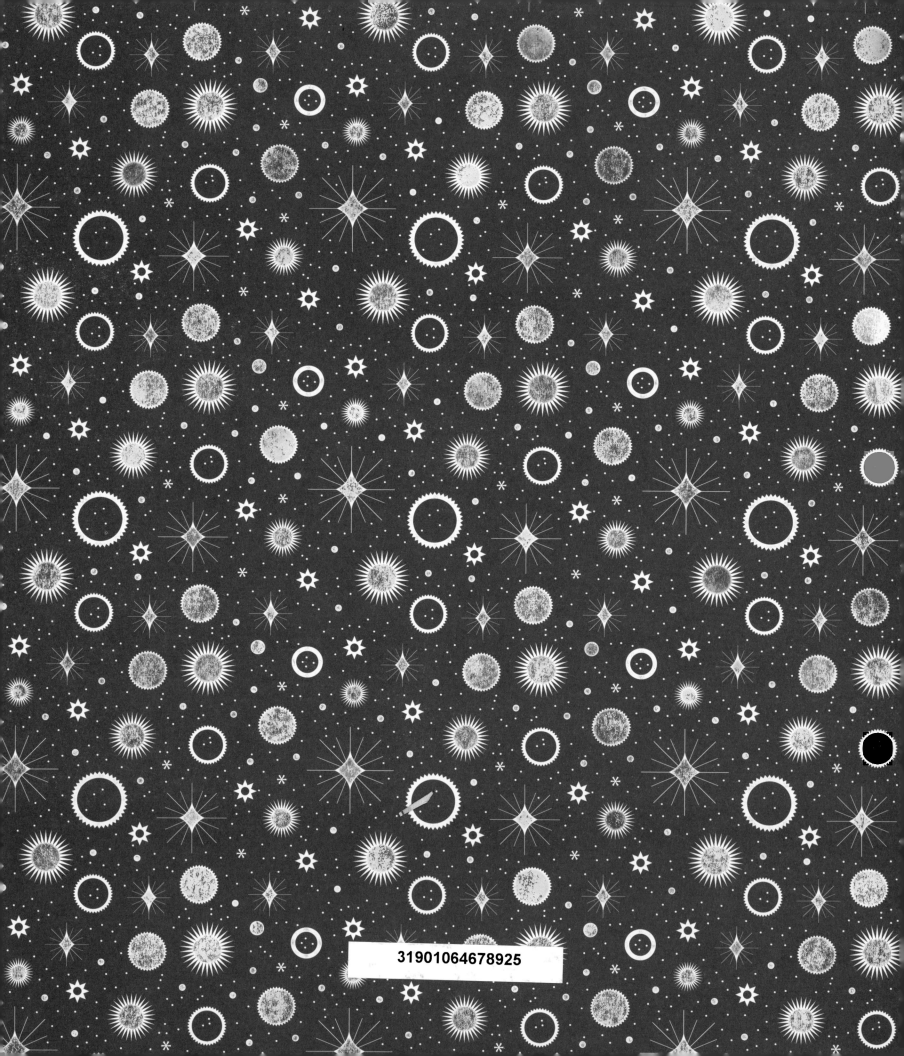